Jn His Presence

30 Days of Devotion, Declaration, Prayer & Reflection

MELISHA BARTLEY-ANKLE

RESTORATION OF THE BREACH
WITHOUT BORDERS

Charlestown, Nevis, W.I

This Journal Belongs To:

_____

_____

. . . .

Published by:
Restoration of the Breach Publishing
Lou-Mot Drive Colquhoun Estate,
Charlestown, Nevis W.I.
restorativeauthor@gmail.com
Tele: (1869) 669-4386

Book Cover Design by:
Nicholas A. Robertson

Formatting and Publishing done by:
Sherene Morrison

Unless otherwise stated Scripture verses are quoted from the King James Bible.

DEDICATION

To Damian and Abbie-Anna Ankle, the loves of my life; and to 'the Girls', who without much effort, have taught me the meaning and importance of true friendship.

ENDORSEMENTS

Melisha Bartley-Ankle, a mentee of mine, has grown and developed into an astute and prolific scholar. In this book, written by her, there is unquestionable value of having a sacred encounter with God- the God she has personally come to know by drawing closer to Him by faith.

In her book you will find a genuine reflection of her personal relationship and favour of God, her chief love.

It is therefore my strong belief that this book, which was birthed from a close relationship with God, will be an ideal tool for those who read as well, as they too will have a closer and an extenuating relationship with God.

Deputy Bishop Phillip N. Salmon
Dr. DD
Jamaica Council Church of God
Seventh Day

I've come to understand that all men must walk in their destiny. This book represents destiny that was in the making for almost two years. Like the Lord told Habakkuk, my dear sister wrote the vision down for almost two years and shared it with us as close sisters through daily devotionals.

We were not only immensely blessed and inspired to start our day but the Holy Ghost spoke through the anointed words carefully written by our sister Melisha.

The power pack precise words presented are always augmented by prayer to transform our lives. This Kingdom inspired book will bless and transform your life.

Savour every moment!

Nicole Barrett
Church of God
Seventh Day Beulah

ACKNOWLEDGEMENTS

The Holy Spirit has a way of pushing us beyond our comfort zone and for that I thank my primary Helper for divine inspiration, especially when I thought "where is God going with this." However, on a daily basis You inspired my mind and I wrote. Additionally, for waking me especially during the times I did not want to get up and also strengthening me when I felt like I did not want to continue with the vision, again all my gratitude to the Spirit of the Lord.

Damian and Abbie-Anna Ankle, you allowed me time and space to get the job done, for that and more I say my family you are super special to me.

To 'the Girls' who long before there was the vision of writing a book, you taught me the value of friendship even amid the distance. Thanks for your constant prayers, love and the joy of sisterhood. Again sisters, I am grateful for the constant push for writing a book; Nicole thanks for the endorsement and I do love you guys.

To Deputy Bishop Salmon, my spiritual father, thanks for your constant prayers, words of affirmation and your endorsement; just a small portion of what you have done for me over the years. In addition, my church family, your prayers, daily reading of the devotionals and encouraging feedbacks were not unnoticed; I must say you assisted in making the dream a reality.

Continuous appreciation to My WhatsApp family group along with everyone else who read the devotionals and sent their commendations, corrections or a better way of wording a sentence I am truly grateful for the invaluable contribution that you have made towards my overall growth; my immediate family and I salute you.

Rev. Leostone Morrison, You came into my life at the opportune time. You saw that it was indeed the birthing season and you would not let up until the manuscript was completed; and even after, you made it possible for the smooth process of the editing and book cover to be completed. Sir, you have given me a new take on what it means to be a Destiny Helper. Although I have known you for a short time, the contribution that you have made in my life cannot be valued monetarily. Heartfelt gratitude to you and your family.

TABLE OF CONTENTS

INTRODUCTION

I have a group of friends called *'the Girls'*. Based on our physical locations and our busy lives, we do not get to physically interact with each other on a regular basis. But amid the distance, we know what it means to have each others' back. We know the importance of treasuring the friendship, that there is the need to strengthen the bond whether by a message or a call, for that is what true relationships require. Like my relationship with *'the Girls'*, we are unable to physically see our Lord and Saviour, and we all have daily activities that compete for our attention. So likewise, it is of paramount importance that we find quality time for our Saviour.

Earlier this year, the Holy Spirit reminded me of the value of early Morning Prayer and having started it is refreshing. Nothing should take away the desire of wanting to spend quality time in the presence of the Lord. Quality time in His presence gives the Lord the opportunity to deposit in us a fresh understanding of His love that will knit our hearts to Him. With such knowledge of His love, 'distance' and 'being busy' will no longer appeal to us as valid reasons for not spending time with God. It may be a few minutes or hours in the presence of the Lord, but once we go with a desire to get more of Him, the encounter will bring joy, peace and revelation.

The thoughts and revelations in this book were birthed from talking with the Lord. As I poured out before Him each morning He downloaded ideas in my spirit; ideas that not only refreshed my soul, but have formed the pages of this book. I pray that as you read each devotional you will enjoy the divine presence of our Heavenly Father.

CHAPTER 1

FAITH

As children of God, we dwell in a kingdom not made with hands. We cannot physically touch or see the operations of the kingdom but we have all been given the key that unlocks all the doors in this domain. God has embedded within all of us a measure of faith, so although in the natural we are in the earth realm, in the spirit, we are already operating from a position of victory. This key called faith is God's gift to us, and has a dual function. First, it serves as currency that affords us the opportunity to sail unchartered waters, unlock and

1

pull desired results into our present situation. Additionally, it allows our minds to become so expansive and expectant that we envision and speak into being the things which to others would seem impossible

GOD'S PERSPECTIVE

* Therefore I say unto you, what things so ever ye desire, when ye pray, believe that ye receive them, and ye shall have them *(Mark 11:24)*.

* Jesus said unto him, if thou canst believe, all things are possible to him that believeth *(Mark 9:23)*.

* But without faith it is impossible to please him: for he that cometh to God must believe that he is, and that he is a rewarder of them that diligently seek him *(Hebrews 11:6)*.

* For we walk by faith, not by sight *(2 Corinthians 5:7).*

* For with God nothing shall be impossible *(Luke 1: 37).*

DAY 1

DO NOT REBUKE THE TESTING

"Immediately the Spirit driveth him (Jesus) into the wilderness. And He was there...tempted of Satan; and was with the wild beasts; and the angels ministered unto Him." (Mark 1:12-13)

Jesus had just been baptized, the Holy Spirit descended on Him, and then God confirmed Him as His beloved Son in whom He is well pleased. So with all that proclamation, one would think the path ahead would be smooth.

However, amid Jesus' ordination for ministry, and prior to the selection of His twelve disciples, the Holy Spirit sent Him to an inhospitable region to contend with wild beasts and temptations from the enemy. It seems difficult or even impossible to believe but this was not the plan of the enemy; but the way God had chosen for Him.

Job 23:10 says "he knoweth the way that I take: when he hath tried me, I shall come forth as gold."

The path of ministry is filled with many rough roads, and like He did with Jesus, the Holy Spirit will lead us into treacherous regions as well, even ones which resemble the valley of the shadow of death. But be not afraid; it is the Spirit that is leading.

The same anointing of the Holy Spirit that kept Jesus, against the threats of wild beasts and temptations by Satan, in the wilderness, is the same Holy Spirit that lives inside of us, and will allow us to not only triumph in our difficult situations, but be perfected for the work God has for us.

DECLARATION

I shall not die in the wilderness,

But I shall

Live to declare the works of

The Lord in the

Land of the living.

DAY 2

LAUNCH OUT AND LET DOWN

...launch out into the deep and let down your nets for a draught." (Luke 5:4)

The disciples had toiled all night but still came up empty. However, as Jesus came on the scene He spoke a statement that would bring life changing results. Note, when Jesus came, He did not ask what was wrong or joined the disciples' pity party, He simply said launch out, get up, change your position. You see the fish that the disciples needed were not at the shoreline, and neither is the breakthrough we seek.

7

All the garbage, the unnecessary things, are washed up at shore; all the complaints and the sinful nature are dominant at the shoreline. But God wants to take us from that place where sin and its enticements have no more control, from the place where the enemy dumps everything on us and we take it, to a higher plain where we are able to stand in Him. He wants to move us to that place where it is complete trust or nothing at all.

It is in the deep, we learn complete dependence on the Father; and it is in that moment of dependence that we will experience His glory- when we realize that all we have is His Word and that is enough to give birth to the blessing.

The disciples went out deeper and the returns blew their minds; we too can experience that kind of blessing. Just tap into God's strength to step away from the shoreline, take that step of unwavering faith, and watch Him move on your behalf.

DECLARATION

Today I take the limits off;

I step away

From the shoreline and

Launch out for

My uncommon blessing.

DAY 3

LEPROSY IS NO MATCH FOR JESUS

"And it came to pass, when he was in a certain city, behold a man full of leprosy: who seeing Jesus fell on his face, and besought him, saying, Lord, if thou wilt, thou canst make me clean. And he put forth his hand, and touched him, saying, I will: be thou clean. And immediately the leprosy departed from him." (Luke 5:12-13)

In ancient time, leprosy was the disease to be feared. It was highly contagious, had no known cure and it literally destroyed the nerve endings of its victim causing them to unknowingly damage their fingers, toes and noses. In the case of the leper, in the above passage, one can assume that he had lost much body tissue, but on that particular day, he chose not to focus on the things that were going wrong. He did not look at the fact that he was dying or that his body parts were falling off, he chose to fix his eyes on Jesus, the author and perfecter of his faith (Hebrews 12:2)

He chose to open his eyes and locking them on Jesus he came to the Saviour, and even, before making his request, he humbled himself at the Master's feet, this, a sign of his understanding that though feared my many, the disease was already subjected to the power and authority of the Father. Note, the leprous man spoke from a position of faith and Jesus honoured his word.

Yes, physical leprosy is not so common in modern times; however, there are things that come to destroy our spiritual nerve endings. There are some situations that arise in the physical-at home-and or at work, that aim to desensitize us from the

11

things of the Spirit. Then there are spiritual attacks such as generational curses that have crippled the entire family thus subjecting them to a life of sin and shame. On the other hand, as Christians we are bombarded with things that tempt us to accept feelings of fear or feelings of not wanting to pray or worship.

Additionally, the enemy brings things that threaten to paralyze our spirits, so even though we know we should be up and about accomplishing different tasks, we just cannot be bothered. The truth is we know some thoughts attacking our minds are unhealthy, but we have no will to fight. However, like the leprous man, let us shift our focus. Yes we are unable to break free on our own, but today let us look to Jesus.

Let us set our gaze on the one who died and gave us the power to be free, the one who wants to take off and destroy every spirit that came to cripple and destroy our souls. Today as we come into his presence, know that whatever the issue, it is powerless in the presence of Jesus, our healing, our deliverance was already bought and paid for, we simply need to take by faith.

DECLARATION

Today every leprous situation,

Every set back, everything that

Would want to render

Me powerless,

I command them to

Die in the presence of the Lord.

DAY 4

EXPANSION IN PAIN

"But the more they afflicted them, the more they multiplied and grew. And they were grieved because of the children of Israel." (Exodus 1:12)

Pharaoh saw the rapid growth of the Israelites, and immediately became concerned as he thought they would become organized and threaten his kingdom. Therefore, in order to prevent such a threat, the Israelites were enslaved. Pharaoh thought slavery would kill their spirits and stop their growth.

15

Through what seemed to be a well thought out scheme, Pharaoh thought he could weaken God's people and eventually break their resolve. He thought that their physical burden would destroy them mentally. But like the pyramids they were building, the Israelites only got stronger and greater.

Understand that the enemy is threatened by our blessing and will do everything in his power to get us discouraged. Let us rise above his tricks and see the trials as machines that we can utilize to build the spiritual muscles needed to successfully accomplish the task. Let us not buckle under the pressure of the enemy or even run away in fear.

Let us be as the eagle in the storm. For the eagle, the storm is what is needful to develop strength in its wings. Therefore, when it knows that the storm is coming, the eagle soars higher and in the path of the storm stretches its wings. It knows its wings will be battered by extremely strong winds; but in the end they will be stronger for the journey. Let us arise in the face of the hardship, stretch our faith in God, and watch as He uses those difficulties to expand our borders. Let us be intentional and grow in our pain.

DECLARATION

Even in this painful situation

I shall

Lengthen my chords;

I shall extend

My borders.

I shall be blessed.

DAY 5

THANK YOU FOR THE TRIALS LORD

"My brethren, count it all joy when ye fall into divers' temptation; knowing this, that the trying of your faith worketh patience. But let patience have her perfect work, that ye may be perfect and entire, wanting nothing." James 1:2-4)

After Stephen was martyred, continuous persecution caused the early Christians to be scattered throughout the Roman world. Seeing that churches were not yet fully established, James, in his letter, sought to comfort the hearts of the believers.

19

James was asking the believers to do the unthinkable. To the ordinary mind it would look foolish and incomprehensible that the people of God were experiencing a time of severe testing, yet James was asking them to welcome the situation - to see it as a teacher and not a destroyer. But what James wanted was that the early church would see the end from the beginning; that they would shift the focus from the pain to see the hand of God working the temptation for the greater good of the church. It was through persecution that the believers fled from Jerusalem into other parts of the world; the dispersed believers spread the gospel wherever they went.

The book of James is calling on the children of God to flip the script just like the early church did during their time of persecution. It is the norm to complain and buckle under the trials, but James is saying 'get excited, rejoice for the temptation has come to teach us that we may be mature and complete before the Father'. Each time the hardship comes, choose to catch a glimpse of the future - see the fruits of steadfastness, perseverance and firm foundation that will be produced from the testing. Yes, our human nature will cry out, but we can take confidence that we are not alone in the storm. Just as the teacher supervises the students during the examination period, Jesus is right there with us in the fire cheering us along.

Let us not despise our periods of hardships. Rather let us ask God to teach us how to worship amid the tears, how to see that difficult times as the instruments He allows to fit us for this life and the life to come.

DECLARATION

Today I refuse to complain.

I refuse to

Be side-lined by trials.

I rejoice for

Everything is working

For my good.

DAY 6

JESUS, HEALER OF INFIRMITIES

"And, behold, there was a woman which had a spirit of infirmity eighteen years, and was bowed together, and could in no wise lift up herself. And when Jesus saw her, he called her to him, and said unto her, Woman, thou art loosed from thine infirmity... And ought not this woman, being a daughter of Abraham, whom Satan hath bound, lo, these eighteen years, be loosed from this bond." (Luke 13:11-12, 16)

Jesus stood in the temple to teach, but as he stood, He was so connected to the Father that He was able to see that within the gathering, there

23

were persons who were not just physically sick, but those who were in need of spiritual deliverance.

For eighteen years the woman in the passage was held in the spirit against her will. She was handicapped; she could not effectively execute the purpose for which God had made her. In addition, in Jewish society it was the common belief of the Scribes and Pharisees that her infirmity has been that she had sinned. Therefore, she was walking under double condemnation - she was bent by an infirmity sent from the devil and she had to contend with the judgmental stares of those who viewed as a sinner.

Like this woman, is there something that for years has held us captive and has made us spiritually handicapped? Are we walking around feeling condemned because of what others think of us? Jesus is still able to sever us from every plan of the enemy. He is still able to take away the pain and give us beauty for ashes, and He is still able to realign our lives.

Understand that even though the woman was handicapped and shackled by feelings of condemnation, she kept on going, she kept pushing, and she kept showing up for duty. She recognized that in her determination to show up for worship, was her deliverance. What has caused us to leave our posts or give mediocre service? What is it we are using as an excuse to not give God our outmost? The woman had reason to be embarrassed, but she kept on going.

Jesus is counting on us to keep on going. He is counting on us to faithfully remain at our posts, for He is the God who honours faithfulness. Let us not complain or get bitter about our lot or what the enemy is doing. Rather, let us continue to serve and to worship with our entire being for God is faithful to deliver and set us free.

DECLARATION

I am set free from every

Known and unknown infirmity.

I willingly do the work that

I have been

Given because Christ

Has set me free.

DAY 7

DO NOT BE AFRAID, JUST SPEAK THE WORD

"And he was in the hinder part of the ship, asleep on a pillow: and they awake him, and say unto him, Master, carest thou not that we perish? And he arose, and rebuked the wind, and said unto the sea, Peace, be still. And the wind ceased, and there was a great calm." (Mark 4:38-39)

After a successful day of teaching, Jesus and his disciples left the multitude to venture on the other side. However, as they went on, a great storm arose and the disciples panicked.

27

Understand that Jesus and His disciples were in the same ship, in the same storm, heading to the other side for the same assignment. However, the disciples' handling of the situation was the complete opposite of Jesus'. According to the scripture, Jesus found such comfort in the storm that he was fast asleep on a pillow. While the disciples were anxious and even spoke destruction over themselves, Jesus was resting.

Jesus was not concerned that the great storm would prevent him from reaching his destination because He knew it was no match for the power and authority that His Father had given Him. Therefore, when He, The Prince of Peace, was awoken by His disciples, He simply spoke His name, Peace, gave the command to be still and creation had to obey. What seemed like a disastrous situation, quickly disappeared when Jesus stood and declared His name and authority.

Recognize that we are blessed to not only have Jesus in our ships - He is also living in our hearts. Hence, when the great storms come to throw us off course, we should not get anxious, speak words of doom or even lose our night's rest just declare the victory and let the Word-Jesus do the work. There is no way the Word can be inside us, in our situation and we perish; He loves us too much to let us fail. Do not panic; the Peace Speaker is our Father, and He is taking us to the other side.

DECLARATION

I stand in my God given

Authority and I

Speak peace to every contrary wind.

I proclaim

That Jesus is in every situation that

I face.

I will not cower in fear but

I will stand and be bold.

DAY 8

GOD WORKS WITH FAITH, NOT OUR STATUS

"And Joshua the son of Nun sent out of Shittim two men to spy secretly, saying, Go view the land, even Jericho. And they went, and came into an harlot's house, named Rahab, and lodged there."
(Joshua 2:1)

In chapter one of Joshua, God reminded Joshua that He had given His people the land. Yet, in chapter two, spies were sent to view the very land that was already promised. On reaching their destination, the men sought refuge at the most unlikely place. However, in that dwelling lived

31

Rahab, a harlot who displayed more faith than the spies and most of the children of Israel.

Rahab's profession did not give her much prestige in society, but her decision to risk it all for God placed her in Faith's Hall of Fame. She hid the spies knowing that she could have been caught and killed. She knew there was a possibility that the men would not return to save her and her family, yet she decided to protect them. Rahab's life was under serious threat but she willingly did it for the God of Israel; the one true and living God.

On the other hand, the spies had first-hand knowledge of what God had done, yet they believed they had to spy out the land. Rahab had only heard about what God had done and is capable of doing, but she looked pass self and declared, *"for the Lord your God, He is God in Heaven above and in earth beneath." (Joshua 2:11)*. While these spies were in the God given land seeking coverage from man, Rahab, the heathen prostitute had the faith to seek protection in the God of the land.

DECLARATION

God, I do not have to see it to believe.

You have spoken

And that is the guarantee.

Your promised word

Shall be made

Manifest in my life.

PRAYER

Father, in the name of Jesus Christ of Nazareth, we come knowing that by faith we are seated with You in heavenly places. As such, we believe that we are already positioned for victory. We rest our confidence in the assurance that even though trials will come we are already victorious in You. Today, we will not become frustrated as we navigate the in- between because You say after we have suffered a while, after we have endured the afflictions, You will settle, strengthen and establish us. You, God, will secure us in a place in You that though the storms are raging we shall not be moved.

Lord, we understand that the road is narrow and filled with uncertainties. But You are God, and You never fail. So we take Your hand and say "yes we will walk with You". Like Peter, we will step out of our boat of sickness, our boat of failure, our boat of affliction, our boat of wanting our own way. We will give our all to You because we know that which You have for us, exceeds that which we could ever think or imagine.

You are the God who delivered our forefathers. You say in like manner as you were with them, so will You carry and deliver us. We turn our eyes of faith and we look to You. As children look to their parents to meet their every need, we look to You believing that You will carry us through in fine style. We trust in You for Your word declares that all things are possible to them that believe.

Today we allow our minds' eyes to envision and bring into the present, the endless possibilities, the inheritance, that You have given us in Your word.

As Joint heirs with Jesus, we declare that we are the lenders and not the borrowers; we are above and not beneath; we are blessed in the city and in the field. You open to us the treasury of Heaven. You give us rain in its season. You bless the work of our hands, and You cause the enemy that rises against us to be smitten before our faces. You are our Abba Father and we know by faith that the answers we await are already delivered.

REFLECTION

CHAPTER 2

TRUST

This is the bold confidence that God will do that which He has promised. Understand that trust is not necessarily the same as faith, which is the gift that we have been given by God. Trust is the end result - the practical things we do in God because He has entrusted us with a gift called faith.

GOD'S PERSPECTIVE

* Blessed is the man that trusteth in the Lord, and whose hope the Lord is. For he shall be as a tree planted by the waters, and that spreadeth out her roots by the river, and shall not see when heat cometh, but her leaf shall be green; and shall not be careful in the year of drought, neither shall cease from yielding fruit *(Jeremiah 17:7-8)*.

* Trust in the Lord with all thine heart; and lean not unto thine own understanding. In all thy ways acknowledge him, and he shall direct thy paths *(Proverbs 3:5-6)*.

* He that dwelleth in the secret place of the most High shall abide under the shadow of the Almighty. I will say of the Lord, He is my refuge and my fortress: my God; in him will I trust *(Psalm 91:1-2)*.

* What time I am afraid, I will trust in thee. In God I will praise his word, in God I have put my trust; I will not fear what flesh can do unto me *(Psalm 56:3-4)*.

* Be careful for nothing; but in everything by prayer and supplication with thanksgiving let your requests be made known unto God. And the peace of God, which passeth all understanding, shall keep your hearts and minds through Christ Jesus *(Philippians 4:6-7).*

Day 9

FOLLOWING DIVINE INSTRUCTIONS

"I will instruct and teach thee in the way which thou shalt go: I will guide thee with mine eye." (Psalm 32:8)

A good teacher must understand his or her content and the learning styles of his or her students; this helps him or her to give proper guidance for optimal results of the teaching and learning process. Our Saviour, the Great Instructor knows that as sheep we are prone to wander. Therefore, He has taken special care to ensure that we stay on the right path. He gives directions that will lead to still waters and restoration. He

43

leads us on the path that He is intimately involved in: He knows all the turns, the potholes, the danger zones, when the path will get slippery and when we are approaching a stop sign.

God wants us to submit to His instructions like David did; He wants us to fully grasp the concept that through the promptings of the Holy Spirit and The Word, He daily guides our thoughts and actions. David, the shepherd boy, understood this very well. As a result, he found intimacy with God as he willingly poured his heart before the Master. He confessed it all - the ups and the downs because he desired the path that God had for him. Each sheep, each journey gets special attention from the Master Shepherd.

Even though it may not look like it, the Lord will lead us to protection and success if we follow Him. The path we are on can be treacherous; but with God as our instructor, we will experience overcoming power if we heed His instructions.

DECLARATION

God, you are the guide of

My thoughts and actions.

I will not make a

Decision without

Consulting You.

DAY 10

DIVINE PURPOSE COMES WITH PROTECTION AND PROVISION

"And the child grew, and she brought him unto Pharaoh's daughter, and he became her son. And she called his name Moses: and she said, because I drew him out of the water." (Exodus 2:10)

Jochebed, Moses' mother, knew of Pharaoh's decree to kill every male child under two years old, but she understood that it was wrong to kill her child. Hence, she did the unthinkable. She used a waterproof basket to place her young child in the River Nile; not knowing what would have happened, she stood watching as the basket

46

floated along. But when it seemed there was no way out, there came Pharaoh's daughter and God used her to give the child a home, his identity and bring him into purpose. She called him Moses, for she pulled him from the waters. In time, God would use Moses to pull His people out of Egypt through the waters of the Red sea.

Jochebed did not know what was waiting in the River Nile, but she knew she had to protect her child. The option that we are faced with seems uncertain, but in order to preserve our purpose we must trust God and step out on the water. The boat is unstable; there are many dangers on the path, but divine protection and provision are also present. Just as God did for baby Moses, our destiny helper will be there right on time to not only pluck us out of troubled waters but provide all the things needed to prepare us for our calling.

Let us trust God to protect and provide for us wherever we find ourselves. The River Nile was no place for a baby, but it opened the door for Moses to be raised in Pharaoh's palace where he had first-hand knowledge of the operations of Egypt. We may be at a place where we are totally helpless and defenseless, we really do not want to be there but that place may hold the key to our divine destiny. So even as we navigate the path that God has chosen for us, even as we walk in His divine purpose, let us rest assured that it does not matter what the rivers of life may bring, our God given purpose is already packed with divine protection and provision.

DECLARATION

Amid the dangers that come

With the assignment,

God is my keeper.

I will not fear what

Man will do to me.

DAY 11

GOD IS BOASTING ABOUT US

"Hast thou considered my servant Job, that there is none like him in the earth, a perfect and upright man, one that feareth God, and escheweth evil?" (Job 1:8)

Job was an extremely wealthy man who could be considered a model citizen; but most importantly he feared, worshipped and obeyed God. Therefore, on that particular day when Satan conversed with God concerning Job, it was not difficult for The Almighty to boast about him. God presented an impeccable profile on Job, he showed the enemy all the things he was doing right; he hated evil, was upright and reverenced God. However, with all the accolades, God permitted Satan to *attack Job in a severe manner.*

"And the Lord said unto Satan, behold, he is in thine hand; but save his life." (Job 2:6)

Job's sincere love for God did not exempt him from the trials of life. God chose to allow the devil access to Job's life because He knew he would remain faithful. God knew that Job loved Him above his family, friends and all his material possessions. He knew Job would not fail the test.

Understand that as children of God, Satan does not have the leverage to do what he pleases with us; but that God, through boasting on us, will allow the enemy limited access to our lives. Yes God will permit Satan to be the author of our trials; but He will always work same for His glory and a deepening of our faith in Him. Let us have the faith not to get flustered in our trials; but let us see the devil as just the instrument that God is using to refine the gold that is on the inside.

DECLARATION

God, my life belongs to You.

Though the trials come,

I will trust in You.

DAY 12

WHO OR WHAT IS MORE IMPORTANT TO US?

"...for the multitude of the people followed after crying, away with him." (Acts 21:36)

Paul arrived in Jerusalem and amid his better judgment, he submitted himself to a Jewish custom in order to maintain peace in the church. However, this decision did not sit well with the Jews. Note, Paul was ministering in the temple, he had done no wrong but the Jews tried to discredit his work, even to have him killed. Similarly, the People had seen Jesus' miracles, He ate with them, comforted their hearts, provided for them,

54

and He did all things well. But they wanted Him dead.

"And they cried out all at once, saying, away with this man, and release unto us Barabbas." (Luke 23:18)

The people chose a rebellious murderer who had nothing to give but suffering; they rejected Jesus who could and wanted to offer everything including life eternal. We may criticize how cruel they were, but do we do the same? We may not verbalize it but our actions may be saying I want Barabbas.

Do we readily accept God's Word of truth? Are we unthankful? Are we convinced that Jesus is our Messiah and that He can satisfy our longings? The answers that stand out will determine what our hearts are saying: whether we are echoing, "all I want is You Lord", or "away with Him".

DECLARATION

God, You are my sovereign Lord.

I want no other God but You.

DAY 13

KNOW WHEN TO GO UP

"And when David inquired of the Lord, He said, thou shalt not go up; but fetch a compass behind them, and come upon them over against the mulberry trees." (2 Samuel 5:23)

When King David heard that he and his men were about to be attacked by the Philistines, he sought the Lord for direction. In verse 19 of the chapter, God gave David permission to go up against the Philistines and he got complete victory over them. However, the second time God denied him permission to go. Note that with victory in sight, David did not have to consult God the

57

second time, but he understood the importance of seeking God at every step of the journey.

It is important to understand that failure to seek God's direction can cause us to err or even lose our lives in the battle. Do not depend on what flesh is saying but, *"trust in the Lord with all thine heart; and lean not unto thine own understanding. In all thy ways acknowledge Him..." (Prov.3:5-6)*.

God knows all the tactics of the enemy and the particular strategy to defeat him. Therefore, let us never go into battle without consulting our Army General. He sees, hears and understands the plans of the opposition even before they are orchestrated. Let us trust Him to tell us if and when to go up.

DECLARATION

All knowing God, You know

The way that

I should take;

I will not make any

Decision without

Consulting You.

DAY 14

GIVE JESUS YOUR SHIP

"And He entered into one of the ships, which was Simon's, and prayed him that he would thrust out a little from the land. And He sat down, and taught the people out of the ship." (Luke 5:3)

Peter and his friends toiled all night without catching a single fish. However, when Jesus appeared on the scene everything changed. Jesus knew that fishing was the source of survival for Peter and his friends. Therefore, after such a long frustrating night, one would think that He would have addressed their basic need- catching fish. However, Jesus seemingly ignored that fact and instead borrowed their boat; this led to a tremendous blessing as the disciples caught so much fish their nets broke.

Like the disciples, we have diligently done what we think should bring success, but it is just not working. Let us stop trying to fix things and simply focus on the task God has given us. Note carefully, it was after the men surrendered their ships to Jesus that they received the blessing.

Similarly, we are required to give God total control of our lives on a daily basis. We must allow the Holy Spirit to use us to bring hope to others. When this is done, God will reveal the blessing. Note, the fish was always there but Jesus wanted the men to perceive their real calling.

Understand that we have no reason to leave God's work unattended to take care of our needs. His word says all things that pertain to life and godliness have already been given unto us (2 Peter 1:3).

God has always taken care of those who faithfully work for Him and He will not stop now. Let Him use our vessels and I assure us that we will reap the reward He has for us.

DECLARATION

God, I give You total

Control of my life:

Use me as

You please.

DAY 15

GOD WILL NEVER SEND YOU AWAY EMPTY HANDED

"And when the day began to wear away, then came the twelve, and said unto Him, send the multitude away...for we are in a desert place. But he said unto them, give ye them to eat." (Luke 9:12-13)

Spiritually, the multitude was full. However, after a long day they needed to feed the physical man. They had a genuine concern but all the disciples could say was, 'turn them away.' They were so caught up with the emptiness around them that they forgot Jesus was in their midst.

The disciples' focus was so misaligned that even when Jesus said, 'give them to eat' they could not grasp the fact that a miracle was on the horizon. They were still concentrating on the little-five loaves and two fish; thus the disciples limited the move of God. We need to take off the limits that restrict what God will do for us. Jesus was not concerned with the fact that they were in a desert place; His focus was ministering to the needs of the people.

Just as Jesus was not perturbed by the lack of bread, our seemingly empty places and difficult situations do not deter God. As a matter of fact, that is what gets His attention. *2 Chronicles 16:9 says, "God's eyes are running throughout the earth to show Himself strong in the lives of those who trust Him".* Picture God on His throne bursting with excitement, waiting for His children to say "God, You are bigger than this; there is nothing hard for

You to handle. Remind this circumstance who is boss."

Understand that when God looks at the situation, He does not see barrenness or impossibility; He sees an opportunity to remind earth of His power and special care.

DECLARATION

God, You are greater than

All my needs.

There is no limit to

What You can do.

DAY 16

THE ENEMY'S SMOKE SCREEN

"And say unto him, Take heed, and be quiet; fear not, neither be fainthearted for the two tails of these smoking firebrands, for the fierce anger of Rezin with Syria, and of the son of Remaliah .Because Syria, Ephraim, and the son of Remaliah, have taken evil counsel against thee, saying, let us go up against Judah, and vex it, and let us make a breach therein for us, and set a king in the midst of it, even the son of Tabeal: thus saith the Lord God, It shall not stand, neither shall it come to pass. (Isaiah 7:4-7)

King Ahaz was crippled with fear as he learnt of the news that the Northern Kingdom of Israel and Syria were planning a total takeover of Judah. Fortunately, through the Prophet Isaiah, God told the King and His people that at that time, the armies would not destroy Judah.

Like Ahaz God sometimes has to tell us to be calm. Stop pacing the floor, stop talking about and maximizing the problem, just stop, pay attention and trust. Yes, the enemy has come breathing threatening words, his weaponry seems well advanced and his army great. But God is saying, "do not work up a sweat or lose your night's rest: everything is under control".

When our backs are against the wall, it is not easy to truly latch our faith unto God's Word. It was hard for Ahaz. But like Ahaz, we do not always see the situation from God's perspective. Ahaz looked at the armies and saw a terrible threat; we view the problem and allow fear to get the better of us. But

Jehovah Gibbor, The Lord Mighty in Battle, saw the armies as two stubs of smoking firebrands. They were just smoke without fire - all talk and no action.

Certainly, the enemy has his plans for the people of God. He attacks at work, in the family, both in the physical and the spiritual; he even seeks to set us up against ourselves. The threats appear overwhelming. However, the Lord of Hosts has come to remind us that we need to take courage and rest in Him. Let us remember that God is in control and even the enemy's best plan will not come to pass - it is just a smoke screen.

DECLARATION

No weapon formed against

Me shall

Prosper and every

Tongue that

Rises against me

I condemn.

PRAYER

Abba Father, our Everlasting God, the kingdom belongs to You. Through the shed blood of Jesus Christ of Nazareth, You, the All Powerful, the All-knowing Go have translated us and made us kings and priests. Lord, as we stand in the heavenly kingdom, we know that in Your presence there is no recession, there is no pandemic and there is no limit to what You desire to do in us and through us, Your children. We know that Your ways are not our ways, and Your thoughts are far greater than ours. So, we trust You today and always to take care of us, to be our guide along the difficult paths of life.

Father the world has become extremely evil, but we depend on You to be our protector. Your word says that You will cover us with Your feathers and under Your wings we can trust. Indeed You have not only shielded us from the snares of the enemy, but Your feathers have kept us throughout the cold onslaughts of life. You have proven that those whose assurance is in You will never go under.

In fact, Your word declares that those who trust in You shall be as Mount Zion, an army base with the best battalion guarding us. We shall not be moved; rather, we shall be planted forever. As Jerusalem is surrounded by mountains, God, You encircle us that the intruder cannot enter our lives. Therefore, we have no need to fear the enemy's smoke screen for You are the God who gives divine protection for every assignment. We will not become anxious; we will rejoice in You.

We rejoice in that there is a blessing to those who trust in You and see You as their hope. According to Jeremiah 17: 7-8, we are like trees planted by the rivers of water, our roots go deep down in You; we pull on Your nourishment and as such our leaves shall not wither from the heat, but we will always be radiant. Though we face persecution on every side, our leaves remain green and our fruit a blessing to all. Father, as You take care of the sparrow and lily in the field, we trust You to take care of us, Your children who were created in Your image and likeness.

Reflection

CHAPTER 3

PROMISE

A promise is an assurance of something happening or that someone will carry out a particular activity. In scripture, God's promises are His assured declarations that something will be accomplished: the binding covenant that the blessings laid out in Holy Scripture has a lifetime guarantee of being fulfilled. This is because the One who gave His word is by nature immutable; there is no shadow of turning in Him.

God's Perspective

77

* Fear thou not; for I am with thee: be not dismayed; for I am thy God: I will strengthen thee; yea, I will help thee; yea, I will uphold thee with the right hand of my righteousness *(Isaiah 41:10).*

* For I know the thoughts that I think toward you, saith the Lord, thoughts of peace, and not of evil, to give you an expected end *(Jeremiah 29:11).*

* When thou passest through the waters, I will be with thee; and through the rivers, they shall not overflow thee: when thou walkest through the fire, thou shalt not be burned; neither shall the flame kindle upon thee *(Isaiah 43:2).*

* Let us hold fast the profession of our faith without wavering; for he is faithful that promised *(Hebrews 10:23).*

* For this is the word of promise, at this time will I come, and Sarah shall have a son. *(Romans 9:9)*

78

DAY 17

THERE IS A PROMISE IN YOUR NOTHINGNESS

"And I will establish my covenant with you; neither shall all flesh be cut off any more by the waters of the flood; neither shall there anymore be a flood to destroy earth...I do set my bow in the cloud, and it shall be for a token of a covenant between me and the earth." (Genesis 9:11, 13)

After the great flood, Noah stepped out of the ark unto a land filled with carcasses; everything and everyone outside of the ark destroyed. As Noah looked on at the vast space of emptiness, God entered into a covenant with Him.

79

The earth laid in ruins, but Noah was given hope. He was given a promise that has not been and never will be broken. Every time it rains, the rainbow is the great reminder that God is not a man that he would lie. In the same manner God made a promise to Noah, He has made a covenant with us.

"Be strong and of good courage, fear not, nor be afraid of them: for the Lord thy God, He it is that doth go with thee; He will not fail thee, nor forsake thee." (Debut. 31:6; Heb. 13:5)

God has proven to be a promise keeper. Hence, we know He will not leave us. Whatever our nothingness may be, God is right in the centre. If it is sickness, he promised to heal; for fear He gives strength; for ashes, He gives beauty; for despair He gives hope. It does not matter how long the list of hopelessness or how dark the night, The Promise Keeper is there. Let us by faith focus on the God who keeps covenants, and not on the seemingly emptiness that life brings.

DECLARATION

Covenant keeping God

You are my rainbow.

You are the One who turns

The nothingness into plenty.

DAY 18

WAIT FOR THE PROMISE OF THE FATHER

"And, being assembled together with them, commanded them that they should not depart from Jerusalem, but wait for the promise of the Father, which, saith he, ye have heard of me." (Acts 1:4)

Jesus was about to ascend into Heaven leaving His disciples to carry out the Great Commission of being witnesses of Him in all nations. However, before they took on the task they were told to wait at Jerusalem for the Promise of the Father.

The First Comforter was about to leave earth; the gospel message had to continue, but Jesus told His disciples to wait at Jerusalem. They were not to get anxious and run ahead of the Word. Instead, they were to stay at the City of Peace: to abide at Mount Zion, the place where God dwells, until they were endowed with power from above.

Note, Jesus had already prayed that the Father would give unto His disciples another Comforter that would abide with them forever. Yet, in order to receive the gift of the Holy Spirit, they had to remain in God's presence. Like the disciples, we are called to be Light Bearers for the Lord. However, before we take on the mandate, before we step out in purpose, we must spend time with the Father. We must have a burning desire to peacefully sit in God's presence in order to receive the needed instructions and power for the journey.

Understand that the disciples had to wait ten days after Jesus' ascension for the Holy Spirit. However, through his empowerment, Peter was able to address an international audience resulting in a worldwide harvest of believers-the first converts to Christianity. Yes, the need may seem urgent and our human nature is telling us to go, but it is imperative that we consult and wait for the leading of the Holy Spirit.

DECLARATION

Though the promise tarry,

It shall not be

Denied; hence,

I will wait for it.

DAY 19

THE SIGNATURE OF GOD

"For we know that the whole creation groaneth and travaileth in pain together until now. And not only they, but ourselves also, which have the first fruits of the Spirit, even we ourselves groan within ourselves, waiting for the adoption, to wit, the redemption of our body." (Romans 8:22-23)

Sin has caused all creation to plunge into a state of moral decadence. Creation cannot truly fulfil the purposes for which it was designed; so devastating is sin and its effects that creation is literally crying out for deliverance. The polluted atmosphere, the destruction of the coral reefs, the

87

contaminated water, everything is just waiting for the day when Christ will return to reinstate all to its former glory.

It is a fact that life has borne some unbearable groaning that has caused our physical bodies to buckle under its pain. Thank God that we can find comfort in Jesus' words to come again to take us unto Himself. He also told us that there will be a new order where this world will be rid of sin, sickness and evil. Therefore, amid the suffering, we have an assurance that we can wait for the promise.

Through the Holy Spirit, also called the first fruit, we have a deposit: the validating signature of God's covenant that we are His children, and we can trust Him to do what he has promised. Through this binding contract, we do not only have a lively hope; we are also constantly comforted that life will not always be like this. There is a guarantee that Jesus Christ who has secured eternal life for us will not only return, but there will be a change in our bodies. No longer will we be subjected to sickness and death, but we will be redeemed, clothed in immortality as at creation.

Thus, as we journey from day to day, let us not conform to the negativities around or even within us. Rather, let us expand our mind-set to the truth that better days will come. As such let us hold on to our earnest expectation.

Declaration

It will not always be like this;

Jesus, You shall return to clothe

Anew our mortal bodies.

DAY 20

HE IS FAITHFUL THAT PROMISED

"Be patient therefore, brethren, unto the coming of the Lord. Behold, the husbandman waiteth for the precious fruit of the earth, and hath long patience for it, until he receive the early and latter rain. Be ye also patient; stablish your hearts: for the coming of the Lord draweth nigh." (James 5: 7-8)

As we navigate the twists and turns of life, there are times when we become overwhelmed. There are times we feel as if this is it: I have no more to give and I really cannot take anymore. Times when we cry, "how long Lord, how long till we sing the glad song?' However, we are

91

encouraged that like the farmer, we should patiently wait for the promise of the Lord.

Note, the farmer knows that in order to get the very best of his crop, he cannot become impatient and reap the harvest before it is fully mature. In the same breath, let us not become edgy. Understand that there are precious souls still waiting to hear that Jesus saves, souls whose hearts are still in need of restoration. Therefore, let us not become weary in proclaiming the good news knowing that the Father's desire is that all comes to repentance.

Like the farmer, we have no room for distractions. We must be vigilant, always on the lookout for the tricks that the enemy will use to discourage. As the farmer waters his field, let us allow the Holy Spirit to water our souls; as he feeds his crop with the necessary nutrients, let us feast on the Word. This way we will not only remain strengthened and settled in God but will also be fruitful.

DECLARATION

I shall remain sober,

Vigilantly awaiting

The promises of the Father.

DAY 21

GOD PROMISES DIVINE PROTECTION

"And the Lord shall sever between the cattle of Israel and the cattle of Egypt: and there shall nothing die of all that is the children's of Israel." (Exodus 9:4)

Although Egypt was again being plagued for Pharaoh's refusal to free the Israelites, God promised that His children would not experience the negative effects of the plagues. God was not only concerned about the lives of His people; He took special care of their properties and everything they owned. Therefore, when all the cattle died in the other parts of Egypt, God placed a covering over the land of Goshen, where the Israelites lived, so that nothing died in that section.

Goshen signifies a land of comfort and plenty. God provided for, comforted and preserved the Israelites' livestock in the midst of the destruction experienced by the Egyptians; He is able to do the same for us, wherever God has placed us - that is our Goshen. As He did for the Israelites, He is more than able to give us comfort and plenty on the job, in our homes; He will also preserve whatever we possess.

God covenanted with Israel to keep them. He kept His Word. Do not become terrified by the threatening pestilence. *"A thousand shall fall at thy side, and ten thousand at thy right hand; but it shall not come nigh thee." (Psalm 91:7)*

DECLARATION

Wherever I am,

I shall prosper.

I shall be kept and protected

By God.

DAY 22

GOD'S PROMISES ARE PUBLIC AND FAITHFUL

"For thus saith the Lord that created the heavens; God himself that formed the earth and made it; he established it, he created it not in vain, he formed it to be inhabited: I am the Lord; and there is none else. I have not spoken in secret, in a dark place of the earth: I said not unto the seed of Jacob, seek ye me in vain: I the Lord speak righteousness, I declare things that are right" (Isaiah 45:18-19)

God has a proven track record that clearly distinguishes Him from idols. He is the one that formed the universe from the chaos at the

97

genesis of time. He is the one that blew His breath, and put His Spirit into man. No one else, no foreign god, could have done what God Almighty has done for His people. Before He formed us, He created a world that lacked nothing, a perfect home for human habitation.

Understand that long before we were born, before we knew we wanted anything, God made a public display of His promises, the inheritance He provided for us. His gift at creation and His continuous promises show that He is a God of His Word: what He says He does. Therefore, when He says, "seek Me, come after Me with your whole heart," his work in the beginning should be a reminder that we have nothing to lose. We will never go after God in vain for He cannot trick us: it is not in His nature.

Psalm 138:2b reminds us that God honours His Word above all His name. Therefore, we have no reason to doubt Him, stand on His promises today and always for He cannot fail.

DECLARATION

I boldly seek after

You God for

I know I shall not

Leave empty handed.

DAY 23

ALL HIS PROMISES ARE YES AND AMEN

"The Lord is not slack concerning his promise, as some men count slackness; but is longsuffering to us-ward..." (2 Peter 3:9)

From the time of the apostles' preaching to the present there are those who continue to scoff at the fact that Christ will return to earth. However, it is not in God's nature to be deceptive. He is unchangeable; He cannot go back on His word. Therefore, whatever He says, however long it takes, it will happen. While our impatience may get the better of us, we must remember God is not governed by time or limitations as we are. God

101

declares His ways are not our ways and His thoughts are not our thoughts (Isaiah 55:8). He is always looking at the bigger picture and the greater good of humanity.

Therefore, as we await His second return, and even the many blessings He has promised in this life, do not become weary or think God is too slow. Do not give place to the enemy who may be saying the grass is greener on the other side and that it makes no sense to trust the Lord. Do not believe the lies; the devil has nothing but pain. In fact the grass that he is bragging about is not even his to give.

Everything in this world belongs to the God of heaven who is always saying trust me. Let us not cast away our confidence which has a great recompense if we endure till the end. It will be worth it after all. Yes, at times life makes it difficult to understand His timetable. Although the battle may become severe and seemingly unbearable, keep on praying, keep on trusting, keep on believing. Giving up or taking a break from the journey cannot be an option. Remember the God who brought us through it yesterday, last week and year by year, still rules and reigns in heaven and earth. He is not slow. He has not forgotten about us; He has not closed His ears to our cries. He has heard and will move at His perfect timing.

God holds His promises above His name. Therefore, He is watching to carry out the Words of assurance that He has given in the Bible; they cannot return to Him void. Trust His faithfulness.

DECLARATION

Impatience will not get

The better of me.

I shall see the manifestation of

The Lord in the land of the living.

PRAYER

Father, Your Word declares that You are not a man that You should lie; it is not in Your nature to deceive Your children. Therefore, whatever You say must come to pass. God, fellow human beings have made us so many promises and have not held true to their words but help us not to judge You based on man's standards. Help us to hold onto the promises that You have given, knowing that You are faithful to carry them through. God, Your name is holy and righteous. Yet You say You place Your Word, your promises, above your name. Thank you for a guaranteed assurance that we can wait on You.

Father, even as we wait, daily renew our faith in You that we will not give up on the Promised Word. Indeed the in between can be long and winding but give us that settled peace that You will not break the covenant. God, in Genesis You told Abraham that You would make his seed multiply as the stars of heaven, and that they would be given all the countries around them; but that word actually took another four hundred years to be manifested. It encountered many challenges and would seem as though it would not happen, but You watched over it and ensured that in the fullness of time it was birthed in the natural. Lord, thank You for the needed anointing to wait on Your fullness of time. Help us not to rush and allow self to tamper with the word, but we will just wait on the God that cannot and will not fail. Father, teach us today and always to stand on Your promises.

REFLECTION

CHAPTER 4

WORSHIP

Worship is ascribing honour to God, recognizing that He is sovereign and we owe our complete existence only to Him. Worship is not just what we do when we gather with our brethren in the sanctuary or that which we do in our devotion time, it is a lifestyle; a way of life that desires to put God first and to be obedient to His will. Everything that we do: the way we conduct business; how we operate on the job, at home, and the way we treat each other, must exude worship.

GOD'S PERSPECTIVE

* God is a Spirit: and they that worship him must worship him in spirit and in truth. *(John 4:24)*

* Although the fig tree shall not blossom, neither shall fruit be in the vines; the labour of the olive shall fail, and the fields shall yield no meat; the flock shall be cut off from the fold, and there shall be no herd in the stalls: Yet I will rejoice in the Lord, I will joy in the God of my salvation. *(Habakkuk 3:17-18)*

* Wherefore thou art great, O Lord God: for there is none like thee, neither is there any God beside thee, according to all that we have heard with our ears. *(2 Samuel 7:22)*

* Come, let us worship and bow down: let us kneel before the LORD our maker. *(Psalm 95:6)*

* And Jesus answered and said unto him, Get thee behind me, Satan: for it is written, Thou shalt worship the Lord thy God, and him only shalt thou serve. (Luke 4:8)

DAY 24

ALLOW JESUS TO TAKE HIS RIGHTFUL PLACE

"It came to pass, as the trumpeters and singers were as one, to make one sound to be heard in praising...saying for He is good; for his mercy endureth for ever: then the house was filled with a cloud." (2 Chronicles 5:13)

Solomon gathered the elders of Israel and arranged for the Ark of the Covenant to be placed in the finished temple. After this was done, the priests and the Levites worshipped God in unison. Understand that the Ark symbolized the presence of God among His people, it was now in the temple and God was pleased. To express His pleasure, God's Shekinah, the glory of His divine presence, overwhelmed the worshippers as they recounted His love and mercy towards them as they travelled through the wilderness.

Then, God dwelt in temples made with hands; but now He desires to live within His people. Knowing this, we must dedicate ourselves to Him on a daily basis. Allow Him to sit on the throne of our hearts and have His way. The priests and the Levites gave their all to God. He showed up among them and took control so their routine had to give way. When our hearts are centered on God in worship, He will show up and show off in our lives.

Psalm 22:3 says " But thou art holy, O thou that inhabits the praises of Israel."

God lives in our praises. Make Him a dwelling place with your praise for He rearranges where He lives. When we make room for God that which we have been struggling to fix for years will be sorted out within minutes because the King of kings, The God of perfection and beauty, is in total control. Let us build Him a house that He may overwhelm us with His presence.

DECLARATION

God, I desire your

Presence more

Than the air I breathe,

So here is my worship - take joy in it.

DAY 25

MAKE THE LORD YOUR DWELLING PLACE

"If ye abide in me and my words abide in you, ye shall ask what ye will and it shall be done unto you." (John 15:7)

Abiding speaks to living or staying with someone for a prolonged period. However, no one would do this with someone that they have little or no relationship. Therefore, for us to abide in Christ and Him in us means a lifestyle of intimacy; an intimacy that comes through the breaking down of barriers, speaking truth in the

116

inward parts, removal of masks, sheets and everything else that would hide our true selves.

You see Jesus has already revealed Himself to us. Psalm 40:7 declares, "lo, I come: in the volume of the book it is written of me." We know Him, but have we made ourselves so vulnerable in His presence that He can say like a husband to his wife, "I know my partner".

In the same manner we only share certain information with our partners or best friends. There are certain secrets or mysteries that are safe guarded for only those who become transparent before the Father. To those of us who make Him our dwelling place, His ways, desires, speech will become so clear that when we make our request we will not ask amiss.

Let us approach God not just as our master, but as our best friend. We will know how to be so on point because in this relationship we are coming to the one who has already revealed His mind to us.

Such revelation allows us to leave His presence with a calm assurance that however He chooses to answer our requests it is for our good and His glory.

DECLARATION

God, my heart is your

Dwelling place.

I live to make You smile.

DAY 26

COME TO THE KINSMAN

"And it came to pass at midnight, that the man was afraid, and turned himself: and, behold, a woman lay at his feet. And he said, who art thou? And she answered, I am Ruth thine handmaid: spread therefore thy skirt over thine handmaid; for thou art a near kinsman." (Ruth 3:6; 8-9)

Empty and broken from the loss of their husbands, Ruth and Naomi returned home to what seemed to be a daunting future. However, on hearing the news about Boaz being a near kinsman, Naomi instructed Ruth to go down to the threshing floor.

Ruth and Naomi thought that Boaz was the nearest relative to help them in their plight. Therefore, Ruth was given specific instructions to go to Boaz at the threshing floor; not to talk or do anything else but to wait for the right cue, then lay at his feet. She did not know what the outcome would be, but as she waited Boaz started a conversation to which she responded, "spread thy skirt over thine handmaid."

Ruth had a need, but as she went to the place of purification and brokenness, she simply waited in silence. We too have needs, but there are times, when we enter into the Holy Place we just need to lay ourselves at the Master's feet and wait. Not going with an agenda telling Him what we want, or what has gone wrong, but just wait. Wait with a spirit that is willing to be broken - a humble heart that will allow the King to initiate the dialogue.

Note that when the King starts speaking His voice will make such a difference that it will relieve our troubled minds. We will experience such peace that we will say like Ruth, "Lord all I need is for You to cover me". Wrap me in your anointing for that is what will break the yoke. I do not want to say anything more than spread the borders of your mantle over me Jesus; like Ruth we will not leave His presence empty handed, our souls will be refreshed and our physical needs met. Today and always our Kinsman Redeemer wants us to just come.

DECLARATION

Father, I quiet myself in your

Presence for it is

Your voice that

Makes all the difference.

DAY 27

GUARD AGAINST THE LUST OF THE HEART

"Who changed the truth of God into a lie, and worshipped and served the creature more than the Creator..." (Romans 1:25)

All of creation declares the creative and majestic power of God. Additionally, His Word gives us a detailed profile of who He is, and His love toward His people. Yet, with the knowledge we have of the Creator, mankind is still searching for "truth" to satisfy their personal desires. Understand that God is the foundation of truth and that will never change. However, the things we

124

watch on television, the music we listen, and society's value systems are constantly bombarding us with things that go contrary to God and His Word.

Therefore, it is imperative that we guard our hearts against the deceptive things that could easily creep in. Note: we may not blatantly say we do not need God, but the things that consume our time suggest that we have not fully acknowledged God as our only source. We have allowed the lust for the things in creation to get the better of us. We allow the world to dictate our lives in such a way that we become success driven before we are Christ driven.

As children of God, we cannot afford to miss the mark. As human beings, we will never be self-sufficient. Hence, we will never get to that place where we do not need God - that place where we can say, "I did it all by myself." We owe our existence, our achievements to God. To permit the standards of the world to consume us, to run after the creature, success, and the riches of life, to put them before the Creator - that is the greatest folly.

Let us be careful regarding the things we permit to motivate us. The little desires left unchecked will corrupt our hearts, tricking us in believing we must spend less time with God in order to get the things of this life.

DECLARATION

I daily put on the breastplate of

Righteousness that I may stand

Against the tricks of the devil.

DAY 28

THE BRIDE OF CHRIST

"Husbands, love your wives, even as Christ also loved the church, and gave himself for it; that He might sanctify and cleanse it with the washing of water by the word, that He might present it to Himself a glorious church, not having spot or wrinkle...but that it should be holy and without blemish." (Eph. 5:25-27)

Marriage between a man and a woman is a direct replica of Christ and the church. In the days of old, oriental brides had to have a ceremonial bath in order to be thoroughly purified for her husband. According to Esther 2:12, for

128

approximately one year, the women contending for royalty were subjected to rigorous beauty treatment as they had to be purified with oil of myrrh and sweet odours before they went into King Xerxes.

Unlike ancient women whose bodies were only prepared with special ointments, Jesus' body went through a different process. He was severely beaten then asked to carry a cross on His fresh wounds, and if those were not enough, He was pierced with nails and swords.

As in the ancient marriage, we - the bride of Christ, were the ones whose bodies should have gone through the process, but Jesus took our place so that we could become a royal priesthood and a holy nation. Understand that we could not save ourselves; but through the washing of the blood of Christ, we are prepared for entrance into His body - the church. In addition, we are sanctified for service through God's Word. Being the bride of

Christ, His Word is our sweet ointment. It is through the Word that we are purified and made spotless from the world. It is only through the Word of God that we can have a sweet odour to perfume the atmosphere.

Only through the Word of God taking deep root in our hearts can our garments remain white. So white that our speech is different, our selfish mean ways disappear, and we are able to love even the unlovable. We boast in salvation and make a positive difference in the world only through Christ - the Word of God.

DECLARATION

God your word is

My anointing

Oil and sweet perfume.

DAY 29

REMEMBER THE GOODNESS OF THE LORD

"And Joshua said unto them...take you up every man of you a stone upon his shoulder...that it may be a sign among you, that when your children ask their fathers...then ye shall answer them, that the waters of Jordan were cut off before the ark of the covenant of the Lord; when it passed over Jordan..." (Joshua 4:5-7)

It was spring and the Jordan River had overflowed its banks. But even as the river stood in its glory, God miraculously parted the waters and allowed the entire nation of Israel to cross over on dry land. However, before they could celebrate and forget about God's kindness, He charged them to build a monument. God wanted His people to remember that the waters were cut off when the priests stepped in with the Ark of the Covenant. Lest they should forget, the stones would cry out that it was not by their might or power; but it was only God. Thus, it was needful for them to guard that memory.

Like the Israelites, we must show constant gratitude. We are alive only through God. The accomplishments, the many miracles, should be a constant reminder that if God had not intervened, if He had not rolled away some troubled waters, we would not have made it to the promise land. Therefore, it is important that we build Him monuments of praise. We should be so addicted to praise that it draws the attention of others.

God commanded the Israelites to remember and tell their children of His goodness. We too must ensure that we do not only treasure what He has done, but that we share such blessings with our children, family members and others in our sphere of influence. Just as the next generation of Israelites did with their forefathers, those who look up to us, must see signs in our lives that prompt them to ask about the meaning of our praise. Our lifestyle should make them want to always hear about the goodness of the Lord in our lives; we cannot tell of the goodness of our God if we do not recognize and remember his workings in our lives.

DECLARATION

I shall forever remember

And talk about

The goodness and

Mercies of God.

DAY 30

DO NOT MISS THE GLORY

"And it came to pass about eight days after these sayings, he took Peter and John and James, and went up into a mountain to pray. And as he prayed, the fashion of his countenance was altered, and his raiment was white and glistering… But Peter and they that were with him were heavy with sleep: and when they were awake, they saw his glory, and the two men that stood with him." (Luke 9:28-29; 32)

Eight days after Jesus told His disciples about the sufferings and death that he was about to experience; He took the inner circle and went to a mountain to pray. While Jesus talked with the Father his appearance changed and His garment reflected the white glory of heaven. Note, It was not when He was performing one of His miracles or in the temple teaching that Jesus was transfigured; rather, it was during sweet communion with the Father.

As Jesus' transfiguration shows, God can grant us a type of transformation; a mountain top encounter. This experience is only birthed when we lock away with Him -when we decide to leave the hustle and bustle, to shut out the distracters, and go deep with the Father. It is during such time that we will undergo a deep change which will be too glorious for explanation: the type of change that will burn the dross and whiten our hearts, making us gems which glisten for Him.

Sincere prayer is the vehicle that allows for transformation in the life of the believer. However, it is worthy to note that during the prayer meeting, when the glory of God was in all its splendour, the disciples fell asleep. The small church had gone to prayer meeting; God came down in His tremendous glory, yet the disciples were heavy with sleep.

The disciples were actively involved in ministry, they were the ones from the inner circle yet when it came to a very crucial point they became sleepy. Let us not be busy with the work of the Lord: feeding the multitude, never missing a service, yet our hearts have fallen asleep. So caught up with everything else, we forego quality time in prayer. We are cheating ourselves out of experiencing or seeing God in all His glory.

Declaration

I shall not be overwhelmed with life;

But, I shall be ready and willing

For the move of God in my life.

PRAYER

Father, as Your bride we chose to worship; we chose to say be enthroned in our hearts. God, we desire to be your dwelling place, for we know that wherever the King of kings lives there is deliverance, power and victory. As we enter into the Holy of Holies, we ask that You spread the borders of Your mantle over us. God, continue to be our refuge and our strength in these trying times. Father, like the woman at the well, we understand that You are the only one who could have given us a new identity. Where we were so embarrassed and thought it was all over, You unshackled us and turned our mess into messages. We honour You for turning things around for us. Thank You for taking us over Jordan and parting the Red Seas of life.

God, we recognize that those seas should have been death traps, but You used them as our walls of protection and allowed us to cross over on dry land. God, yet even after You delivered us, we allowed ourselves to be cumbered with the cares of life. We stepped away from your glory and got distracted by the sugar coated things the enemy dangled before our eyes - things that caused our feet to almost slip, but You stepped in just on time. When we thought it was all over your mercy snatched us and gave us another chance. For that we pause to worship, and to reflect on your never failing love and goodness.

Father, we come with our alabaster box and we pour out the oil of our worship before Your throne; we pray that it will be a sweet smelling savour that rocks You on Your throne. Lord, let our hearts beat with gratitude for all that You have done and continue to do as we navigate the challenging turns of life.

REFLECTION

DESIRE OF THE HEART

I pray that we will not deprive ourselves of the comfort and peace of mind that is found only in God. As the heart panteth for the water brooks, so let us daily desire the never ending flow of the presence of our Father.

Let us recognize that this is the only flow that will build our faith and trust. May we take hold of His promises and worship continually before His throne.

ABOUT THE AUTHOR

A graduate of the Universidad de Montemorelos, Melisha believes that with a renewed mind and God by her side, there is no limit to what she can achieve. Mother of an energetic daughter, wife, missionary and an educator, this Jamaican, has a passion for God and for excellence. Additionally, she lives by the mantra, "a fulfilled life is one that is given in service to God and her fellowman."

www.ingramcontent.com/pod-product-compliance
Lightning Source LLC
Chambersburg PA
CBHW072009040426
42447CB00009B/1557